What Others Are Saying

"I felt affirmations and visu_____ ____ _ ___a ot empty happy thoughts that didn't work, until I used them in a competition for World Champion of Public Speaking--and won! Everyone should know about the tools you share."

– Darren LaCroix, 2001 World Champion of Public Speaking

"Powerful and life changing. Jodi puts things into perspective so anyone desiring to improve their quality of life or relationship can do so. *Dynamic Affirmations* is packed with insight and all the tools anyone needs to improve."

– Tony Ash, Self-made Corporate Exec

"Jodi's message is so practical and inspiring, it's changing lives one at a time."

– Anna Pansino, Successful Investor

Dynamic Affirmations

Learn to Live the Law of Attraction with Purpose and Passion

JODI SANTANGELO

If self-help isn't helping and you've given up on
affirmations that aren't working for you,
the powerful tools in this book guide you through
the proven steps to achieving your desires
and living the life you always dreamed of.

New York

Dynamic Affirmations

Learn to Live the Law of Attraction with Purpose and Passion

Copyright © 2010 Jodi Santangelo. All rights reserved.

No part of this publication may be reproduced or transmitted in any form or by any means, mechanical or electronic, including photocopying and recording, or by any information storage and retrieval system, without permission in writing from the author or publisher (except by a reviewer, who may quote brief passages and/or short brief video clips in a review.)

Disclaimer: The Publisher and the Author make no representations or warranties with respect to the accuracy or completeness of the contents of this work and specifically disclaim all warranties, including without limitation warranties of fitness for a particular purpose. No warranty may be created or extended by sales or promotional materials. The advice and strategies contained herein may not be suitable for every situation. This work is sold with the understanding that the Publisher is not engaged in rendering legal, accounting, or other professional services. If professional assistance is required, the services of a competent professional person should be sought. Neither the Publisher nor the Author shall be liable for damages arising herefrom. The fact that an organization or website is referred to in this work as a citation and/ or a potential source of further information does not mean that the Author or the Publisher endorses the information the organization or website may provide or recommendations it may make. Further, readers should be aware that internet websites listed in this work may have changed or disappeared between when this work was written and when it is read.

ISBN 978-1-60037-693-1

Library of Congress Control Number: 2009934412

MORGAN · JAMES
THE ENTREPRENEURIAL PUBLISHER

Morgan James Publishing, LLC
1225 Franklin Ave., STE 325
Garden City, NY 11530-1693
Toll Free 800-485-4943
www.MorganJamesPublishing.com

In an effort to support local communities, raise awareness and funds, Morgan James Publishing donates one percent of all book sales for the life of each book to Habitat for Humanity. Get involved today, visit www.HelpHabitatForHumanity.org.

Table of Contents

PART IV: Focus for Greater Results

PART V: Dynamic Tools for Accelerated Results

PART VI: Bonus Chapter

"I deserve good things.
I am entitled to my share of happiness.
I refuse to beat myself up.
I am an attractive person.
I am fun to be with."

– Daily Affirmation with Stuart Smalley,
Saturday Night Live

Welcome!

What are the ways you are now seeking to reach your goals?

Maybe you're one of the many people who are working 18 hours a day in a frenzied attempt to get ahead and realize your dreams.

Perhaps you write out goals each year to achieve success, good health, or your ideal body weight, and end up frustrated because what you want is not showing up in your life.

Chances are you've been told to use positive thoughts and statements or establish intentions, and you thought that would make you feel better. But you're still unfulfilled.

Maybe you've even tried affirmations to attract what you want. And that's what--self-confidence? The perfect mate? Prosperity? Or have you given up, thinking affirmations are a waste of time?

You just don't know how to get what you want and achieve a joyful, satisfying life.

You're not alone. Many people are caught in this cycle of frustration and discontent. They use goals or intentions, affirmations or mantras, wishing and hoping for more but eventually giving up, thinking such things are a waste of time.

If you're sick and tired of using these methods that frankly don't work for you, this book will save you years of more frustration.

> **Key point: The information in this book is key to your making positive changes in your life so you can get what you want with better, faster results.**

Have doubts?

I did, too. I spent years searching for ways to achieve my desires. I read all the books, bought the tapes, went to seminar after seminar-all this positive thinking stuff-but with no results.

Then, all of a sudden, the answer was right in front of me.

There was no denying it. What I discovered is as true as a science. A universal law! You'll see.

Now it's your turn.

What you're about to learn transcends positive thinking and self-help information.

At last, you are about to learn the science behind methods such as goals and affirmations and understand why yours might not be working for you.

Want to be a money magnet? Wildly successful? Have the relationship of your dreams?

Start now to get the results you deserve!

Your Step-by-Step Action Plan To Get Results!

The information contained in this book will bust through any barriers you've had about affirmations up until now. You'll become an expert at creating and using *Dynamic Affirmations* to create your new life experiences. However, please note this program is not intended as a textbook to read in one sitting. It's a hands-on learning process which requires that you actively participate in the exercises, giving yourself time to work through each one.

- Discover tips, tools and scripts to create and accelerate your affirmations.

- As your mind triggers insights, record your thoughts.

- Doing something with the information you learn is key to your success. If you follow the program as outlined (meaning, without skipping ahead and missing key points), and if you take action as suggested and implement the tools, you'll quickly change the way you court success, and you will catapult your life and business to new heights!

Clarification of terms:

I'd like to familiarize you with a few terms in case they are new to you.

affirmation: A short positive statement spoken in the present tense.

attraction effect: The effect of the Law of Attraction.

inspired action: Action that comes from within as opposed to being told what to do. It's that excited feeling you get to do something when you are passionate about what you're doing or being.

mini-movie: A brief series of actions we create in the mind and visualize as if we're acting out a scene in a play or movie.

vibe: (short for vibration) The energy we radiate as a result of our emotions, positive or negative.

vision board: A vision board (also called a collage, wish, or dream board) is typically a poster board on which you paste images you've torn out from various magazines. You paste images of what you want to attract in your life and usually hang it on a wall.

Part I:

Positive Statements, Goals And Affirmations.
All Created With The Same Intent;
To Bring You What You Want

What Is An Affirmation?

The term "affirmation" may be new for you. There are several terms people use interchangeably, such as intentions, mantras, positive statements, goals, and others, but regardless of what you call them they are created for the same reason: to bring you everything you want--relationships, material objects, situations and events--whatever you believe will make you feel better by having it.

What exactly is an affirmation? According to the experts, it's a short, positive statement spoken in the present tense that makes you feel good or declares a desire.

Key point: An affirmation is a statement spoken in the present tense that declares a desire.

Affirmations are:

- **Positive**
- **Short**
- **Personal**
- **Present tense**

Motivational experts agree that the fastest way to get what you want is by using affirmations. **Affirmations are among the most powerful tools for personal transformation.**

Did you ever see the *Saturday Night Live* skit "Daily Affirmation with Stuart Smalley"? Stuart Smalley is a new-age, self-help guru who gives himself a pep talk in his full-length mirror and repeats positive statements such as: "I'm good enough, I'm smart enough, and dog-gone-it people like me."

Does this sound familiar? Maybe you're like the millions of people who use affirmations to feel better and get what they want. Some want the perfect job and a large bank account, while others affirm a slender or healthy body.

Have you written your own affirmations over and over on a yellow pad or on sticky notes that you put on your mirror or computer? Perhaps you've hung 3 x 5 affirmation cards on your refrigerator with a magnet or tucked them on the dashboard of your car, only to take them down because they didn't seem to work.

If affirmations are supposed to be so powerful, why don't they always work?

If you're tired of standing in front of the mirror repeating affirmations that haven't been working for you, you're about to discover why.

You'll soon understand why affirmations don't work for *most* people.

Notice I'm not saying *all* people. You may enjoy reading and affirming inspirational sayings, or passages from the bible, or famous quotations that motivate you and make you feel good. If that's the case and they make you feel good, keep using them.

I have to admit, though, that at one time my affirmations weren't working for me. I was ready to give up on myself. Then something happened and I suddenly got it! I finally understood *why.* You will too.

My discovery is so powerful and exciting, I'm convinced you'll get a huge "Ah ha!" from what I'm about to share with you.

Haven't you lost enough time already?

What Methods Are
You Now Using?

Let's start by checking in.

What positive statements, goals or affirmations have you been using?

Exercise: Follow the instructions below, then list all of your current methods (positive statements, goals or affirmations) in the space provided.

1. Think back to methods/affirmations you've used in the past and list them below. Check "current" if you are using them now.

2. Feel free to include a new affirmation that may apply to your life today, something you would like to attract.

3. After you list your methods/affirmations below, ask yourself whether they came true for you or you gave up on them because what you wanted didn't show up in your life? Please check either "Came True" or "Gave Up."

4. _____

_____ Current _____ Came True _____ Gave Up _____

5. _____

_____ Current _____ Came True _____ Gave Up _____

6. _____

_____ Current _____ Came True _____ Gave Up _____

7. _____

_____ Current _____ Came True _____ Gave Up _____

8. _____

_____ Current _____ Came True _____ Gave Up _____

9. _____

_____ Current _____ Came True _____ Gave Up _____

10. _____

_____ Current _____ Came True _____ Gave Up _____

PART II:

When Affirmations Don't Work.
The Facts No One Is Telling You

The Attraction Effect
The Law Of Attraction

To understand why affirmations don't always work, it's important to understand the Law of Attraction, the science of getting what you want.

Maybe you've heard about the Law of Attraction from the best-selling book and hit movie *The Secret*, or from the movie *What the Bleep*.

Or perhaps you're familiar with expressions used to describe the Law of Attraction, such as "you reap what you sow," "birds of a feather flock together," or "when it rains it pours." You've probably even caught yourself saying, "Wow, what a coincidence!" or "it came from out of the blue," and "they're so lucky." These expressions are examples of the Law of Attraction in action!

> **Key point: The real reason your affirmations may not be working for you comes down to a science, a universal law of cause and effect called the Law of Attraction.**

How does it work?

To understand how it works is to know that everything in our vast universe is energy, including you, me, our thoughts, and our emotions. We're constantly radiating energy (commonly known as a vibration, or vibe, for short), and the type of energy being radiated is determined by our emotional state. Of course, our emotional state or feelings vary from hour to hour and sometimes minute to minute.

All feelings cause us to send a vibe positive or negative.

Some feelings that cause us to generate positive vibes include:

Love

Joy

Happiness

Appreciation

Gratitude

Excitement

Peacefulness

Confidence

Pride

Some feelings that cause us to generate negative vibes include:

Anger

Worry

Blame

Frustration

Shame

Guilt

Sadness

Fear

Confusion

What's important to know is this: For every feeling or emotion we have we unconsciously emit a vibe, positive or negative, every moment of our lives.

That's when the Law of Attraction comes in:
The theory behind the Law of Attraction is that energy attracts like energy. It's a matcher of vibrations. When you're feeling good you put forth positive vibes. The Law of Attraction matches that vibe by bringing you more of the same positive energy. When you're feeling bad, the Law of Attraction matches that, too.

> **Key point: The Law of Attraction has only one job: to match the vibrations you send by giving you more of the same vibe.**

You've seen this principle in action. Think of someone you know who is always positive and upbeat, and everything seems to go their way. We call them lucky! You also know people who are negative, critical, and always have something to complain about. Each type of person reflects the results of the energy they give off.

You are like a living magnet, always attracting what you want, as well as what you don't want.

The Law of Attraction is not a "decider." It doesn't know if the vibe you're sending is good for you or bad for you, healthful or not, or even if you want it. It's only a "matcher," and it gives you more of what you are sending.

It starts with your thoughts, but it is so much more than a thought. The Law of Attraction responds to your emotions and whatever you're FEELING.

Whatever you are feeling--and therefore vibrating--the Law of Attraction is delivering. Your emotions are always creating the events in your life.

**What does the attraction effect have
to do with affirmations?
Everything!**

When Affirmations Don't Work And Success Is A Secret

My affirmations never worked for me, until one day I had my "Ah ha! life-changing" moment.

My personal story speaks volumes about my experience with affirmations and why I was convinced they didn't work.

Though I don't often look back, sharing my experience may help you learn why your own affirmations might not be working.

Here's my story:
In the early 1990s everything seemed to be going my way. I was married, lived in a beautiful home in a town near the ocean, and had a career I loved that allowed me to travel the world. In 1992 I got my wake-up call. The caller seemed to say, "Things are going too well for you, your life is too darned good, now it's time to pay up." Everything began to unravel. After several unsuccessful attempts at starting a family, my marriage eventually dissolved, I was laid off from the job that I loved, and out of the blue I developed a serious life-threatening illness.

This illness was systemic, and even today is something of a mystery. So I was already feeling really low, when a number of disabling physical symptoms set in.

As you can imagine, it was a horrible period for a young adult, and I was experiencing and expressing major negative emotions. All I could think of was poor me, woe is me, and why me? I was frustrated, angry and resentful. I was thinking about how bad I felt and talking about my illness over and over, and hadn't yet learned that I was really attracting more bad feelings. I didn't realize that the Law of Attraction always matches our emotions.

Learning the secret

Often, it's the time when we hit rock bottom that real change occurs. I looked to seek relief and began to take responsibility for my own healing. I read and listened to everything positive I could get my hands on. I practiced what I call "self-care" and it was during this period of tremendous growth that I learned about affirmations. The self-help books claim that affirmations can be powerful tools for personal transformation, so reaching for anything to make me feel better, I wrote an affirmation on a sticky note and put it on my mirror. It said, "I am healthy."

Morning, noon, and night, this affirmation became my mantra: "I am healthy."

At the time I was still going through extensive treatment that left me sick for days. Praying for anything to make me feel better, I'd lift my head up long enough to look in the mirror and say my positive affirmation, "I am healthy." As I looked in the mirror, I'd notice a new clump of hair missing, all the while continuing to repeat over and over, "I am healthy. I am healthy. I am healthy."

And what do you think was going through my head?

"Yeah, right, that's not true. I'm not healthy. That's a lie. Look at me. I'm sick! It's not fair!"

Then I'd keep going on this negative spiral. Ever notice how one negative thought breeds another, and yet another? I became totally depressed even as I stated my positive affirmation.

Yet I was *feeling* awful. What vibe is that, positive or negative? Most definitely negative!

I became aware that saying "I am healthy" actually *felt* bad. I was making a *positive statement* that had a *negative vibration!*

That was my "Ah ha!" moment, the epiphany, the pivotal event that changed my life.

What was the Law of Attraction responding to? The negative emotion and negative energy I was vibrating.

Of course I was depressed as I said my positive affirmation because I kept going through my day sending negative vibes. No wonder I was sick for so long!

The Law of Attraction didn't know or understand that I wanted to be healthy. It was only responding by matching my negative emotions and doing a really good job! Saying "I am healthy" didn't feel good, and I was only attracting more of what I didn't want.

Key point: The Law of Attraction doesn't respond to my affirmation. It responds to how I *feel* about the words I use to create my affirmation.

All the frustration and time I'd spent on affirmations that didn't work, and it all came down to simple principle.

Here's what I learned: In order to work, my affirmations must be *true for me* and make me *feel good*, and your affirmations must be *true for you* and make you *feel good*. This is the critical information the self-help books left out!

Your words need to match your *feelings*.

Remember that the Law of Attraction is always checking to see how you're *feeling*, then it responds by giving you more of the same vibration.

Affirmations Are Not Created Equal

Affirmations are not created equal

Affirmations can have different vibrations for each of us. You might say the words "I am healthy" and that may feel good for you, while for me, struggling as I was with my health, the contradiction brought about a negative vibration. Affirming that I love my job feels really great to me, though the same statement may trigger a different vibration for you. The same affirmation can feel very different for each of us. And if we are already enjoying financial abundance most likely we wouldn't write an affirmation to acquire wealth. In many circumstances, some affirmations are bound to contradict some people's truth.

Let's look at some **common affirmations** and the questions to ask yourself to determine how you *feel* about the words being used:

- **I love my job.** *When does that feel good? When it's true!*

- **I am healthy.** *How does it feel when you say the words?*

- **My business is successful.** *When is that true? When my business is successful!*

- **I'm successful in all that I do.** *Can you believe that and feel good about this statement?*

Now you know *why* your affirmations may not be working—they don't match the way you are feeling. However, your affirmations can work; we just need to keep tweaking them until they *feel good* to you!

Remember, the Law of Attraction doesn't respond to your words but to the way you *feel* about them.

Think about what you have been affirming over and over that really doesn't feel good.

Health? Career? Relationships? Body image? Self-Confidence? Money? Success? Fame?

Exercise: Take the same methods/affirmations you recorded earlier and describe how you really feel about each.

1. Affirmation: _____

How does it feel? _____

2. Affirmation: _____

How does it feel? _____

3. Affirmation: _____

How does it feel? _____

4. Affirmation: _____

How does it feel? _____

5. Affirmation: _____

How does it feel? _____

Tips to help you create affirmations that will work for you

- In order to work, your affirmations must be *true* for you and *feel good* to you.

- The words need to match your feelings.

- The Law of Attraction doesn't respond to your words; it responds to the way you feel about the words.

- The Law of Attraction is always checking to see how you feel, and always responding by giving you more of the same vibe.

This is the secret of attracting what you want!

Part III

Critical Tools For Getting Results

Creating And Rewording Affirmations
So They Work For You

The following section gives you specific tips, tools, and scripts for creating and rewording your affirmations.

Exercise: Please fill in the blanks below to review the important principles learned so far.

1. The key to making an affirmation work is to make it
_____ for me!

2. My words need to match _____.

3. The Law of Attraction responds to _____
_____.

Answers: 1) true, 2) match my feelings,
3) how I feel about the words.

Tool #1:

Don't Doubt Your Affirmation

Pretending that you believe your affirmation doesn't always work.

Do you feel you're telling yourself a lie as you repeat your affirmation in front of the mirror? Are you writing and saying empty happy thoughts over and over?

Example: If you tell yourself that you earn a whopping income this year, are the top sales person in your industry, or have an attractive body--but you don't *feel* you do or don't believe you can really have it, you can't fool the Law of Attraction. It responds only to how you are thinking and *feeling.*

If you're doubtful or skeptical, don't pretend, as I had, that you do not feel negative emotions. The Law of Attraction is checking to see how you're really feeling, then giving you more of it.

Let's explore how some affirmations might not feel good, while other affirmations are just not believable. In many cases you may experience both emotions.

Exercise: Answer the following questions in the space provided.

1. What have I been affirming that I really don't believe, such as: "I am a millionaire," "I live in the house of my dreams," "I am successful," or "I'm with my ideal partner"?

   _____

   _____

   _____

   _____

   _____

2. Any idea why you don't believe your affirmation?

   _____

   _____

   _____

   _____

It's possible that you don't believe your affirmation because of old patterns or beliefs. The Belief Buster tool in the next exercise will help you uncover beliefs that may be stuffed in your subconscious.

3. What affirmations don't feel true for me?

Example: Having repeated "I am healthy" didn't feel true or good to me because at the time I had evidence that I wasn't healthy.

_____

_____

_____

_____

_____

Using the tools in the following chapters will help you write affirmations that feel better for you.

Tool #2:
Bust Through Limiting Beliefs

Do you believe you can have the relationship of your dreams, the financial abundance you deserve, or the success you desire? If truly believing in your success is a huge leap for you, you might have deep-rooted, subconscious limiting beliefs blocking you, cancelling out your affirmations and sabotaging your goals.

Example: All beliefs come from our past--from our teachers, our families, and our own experiences. These early beliefs can have a powerful effect on how we think and feel and respond to situations. Some beliefs work to our benefit while others limit us from attaining all that we desire.

> **Key point: Everything we do stems from our beliefs. Some of those beliefs are *limiting* beliefs.**

Here are some examples of beliefs that can affect us negatively:

- I have to work hard to make money.
- Money is the root of all evil.

- It's not spiritual to make money.

- Don't stand out in a crowd.

- Don't get too excited--you wouldn't want to be disappointed.

- Play it safe. Only fools take risks.

Do any of these beliefs ring a bell for you? The best way to identify your own limiting beliefs is to listen to your conversations. They'll come after the "yes buts" and after the word "because."

Example: Someone tells you that you look great today, and you answer, "Yeah but you should see me in a bathing suit." This kind of statement indicates a limiting belief around weight or self-image. Or you say, "I can't have that career because I don't have a college education." That kind of statement suggests a limiting belief that you're not bright enough or are undeserving.

Exercise: Answer the following questions in the space provided.

In conversations with others or in my own self-talk, when do I say "yes but" or follow "because" with a negative reason?

1. _____

2. _____

3. _____

4. _____

5. _____

Other ways to uncover your limiting beliefs is to ask yourself a question, then write the answer. Just write and write and write, without analyzing or filtering out your thoughts as they come up.

Example: Here's what I think about money: relationships, success, abundance, health, weight, career, fame, or another issue you struggle with.

_____

_____

_____

_____

_____

Now go back to the list of 5 limiting beliefs you recorded and ask yourself, "Is that really true?" Or, "It may have been true in the past but is it still true today?" "Who says it's true?"

_____

_____

_____

_____

_____

Often, the act of uncovering the limiting belief and simply setting the belief on paper and out of your head is enough to take the negative charge out of the belief and defuse it. The emotion we invest in each limiting belief is what attracts the results we don't want.

The good news is that a belief is just a thought that became a habit repeating itself over and over, and we can choose to replace it at any time with a new, more beneficial thought. How? By continuing to uncover the blocks that limit your success and to create *Dynamic Affirmations* that work for you!

Tool #3:

Focus On What You Want, Not What You Don't Want

Positive statements aren't always positive.

Example: Often, we think we know what we want but we express it in terms of what we don't want. For example: If we're in a state of poor health, affirming "I don't want to be sick" has a negative vibe attached to it. It doesn't feel good, and the Law of Attraction can only match that negative vibe and bring you more.

Other common negatives include:

"I don't want to be overweight."

"I don't want to lose my job."

"I don't want to be in a controlling relationship."

"I don't want to be broke."

"I don't want to be alone."

"I don't want this, I don't want that."

> **Key point: We think we know what we want, but we end up creating affirmations and setting goals for what we don't want.**

Expressing what you don't want is easy. What we really want is the opposite; to experience good health, a slender body, a satisfying career, an ideal relationship, wealth, great friendships, and so on.

The secret to succeeding in reaching your goal is to ask yourself what you do want, then create a positive statement rather than a negative statement. When you reframe your affirmation in a positive manner, it feels better and sets the energy in motion to attract what you want.

Exercise: In the space provided, make a list of the "don't wants" you've experienced in the past or "don't want" today. Examples: Career, health, abundance, relationships, etc.

1. _____

2. _____

3. _____

4. _____

5. _____

Now, reframe your negative affirmations. Write them again in terms of their opposite or what you *do* want.

1. _____

2. _____

3. _____

4. _____

5. _____

When your words change from negative to positive, your vibration changes and your results will change.

Learn to tap into your body and feel the difference between a low- frequency and a high- frequency vibration. This feeling serves as your vibration indicator, always letting you know if you're attracting what you want--or more of what you don't want.

Tool #4:

Distinguish Between "Want" And "Should"

How passionate are you about your desires?

Do you really *want* that thing you're asking for? To get it you must really want it. Sometimes what we think we "should" have, do, or be, we disguise as a "want." You'll recognize this *attempt at pretense* if you lose enthusiasm for doing your affirmations.

Example #1: My father said I should continue the family business. I'm inspired to become a professional golfer.

Example #2: Mary wanted a sports car like her friends had, but she is also environmentally conscious. Because she's more concerned about being energy efficient than keeping up with others, *wanting* a sports car didn't really *feel good*. Eventually it dawned on her that what she really wanted was a hybrid car. Since her messages to herself were conflicting, most likely she would never get that sports car. She was in alignment with the hybrid. The hybrid she could get excited about!

> **Key point: Focus on how you *feel*. Strong emotion causes the experience!**

Exercise: Make a list of ways to finish the sentence: "I should…"

1. _____

2. _____

3. _____

4. _____

5. _____

Next, go through the above list and ask yourself why you feel you should. Is each item something you really want or something you feel obligated to have, do, or be?

1. _____

2. _____

3. _____

4. _____

5. _____

If you're stuck and don't see how it's possible to have what you really "want," find things to appreciate about where you are now and look for benefits from what you feel you "should" do. This kind of positive outlook will lessen the resistance you experience and allow other opportunities to appear.

Example: Phyllis really wanted to be in a position that would allow her to volunteer at helping more people in her community. However, she knew she "should" work full-time to provide for herself and her son. By maintaining her desire and her affirmation, she was soon promoted to a position in her company heading up its volunteer programs. A perfect fit!

When you're coming from a place of peace (without resistance) and have a strong desire, and you are flowing positive energy toward that desire, the Law of Attraction is matching your emotion and bringing you more of the same.

If you're writing affirmations that you don't have a strong desire for, those pseudo "wants" might never materialize. The Law of Attraction is always responding to how we really feel.

Tool #5:

Make Your Wants Exciting And Believable

Each affirmation should be big enough to be exciting but realistic enough to be believable to you.

When you read an affirmation aloud, what *feeling* does it evoke?

Positive Vibes: Your affirmation must be about something important to you to stir you, get you excited, cause you to daydream and talk about your desire. These behaviors feel good, and the Law of Attraction responds by sending you more good feelings.

Negative Vibes: If your affirmation is too big, unrealistic, or unimaginable, your disbelief in its attainment feels bad, and the Law of Attraction responds by sending you more bad feelings.

> **Key point: Whatever you're *feeling*, the Law of Attraction is matching and therefore delivering!**

Example: Say you have the long-range goal of becoming the CEO of a large company, or you desire to lose a lot of body weight. The affirmation for such a major goal feels overwhelming. Consider dividing your goal into smaller interim steps and smaller affirmations until your longer-range goal feels more attainable.

Write your new affirmation for this exercise below. Then circle the responses most appropriate for each.

How do I feel about each affirmation?

1. _____ Exciting   Believable

2. _____ Exciting   Believable

3. _____ Exciting   Believable

4. _____ Exciting   Believable

5. _____ Exciting   Believable

Tool #6:

Give Your Affirmations A New Beginning

Thoughts and words create emotion

If you feel good stating an affirmation as if you already have what you want, and you can stir up strong positive emotion for it, keep doing what you're doing. The subconscious mind doesn't know the difference between having what we want and pretending that we already have it. The Law of Attraction doesn't know either. It is a universal law, and its only job is to match the feelings evoked by our thoughts and words.

If changing your words around would feel better to you, try beginning your affirmations using one of the following:

"I'm in the process of"

"I am becoming"

"I am creating"

"I am willing"

Example: "I'm in the process of attracting my ideal job." "I am becoming healthy." "I am creating a relationship." "I am willing that _____." After each statement ask yourself, "Does it feel true?"

You want to be able to reply, "Yes, I am in process of attracting my ideal job. I'm sending out résumés." Or, "I'm networking." Or, "I'm following up on referrals." In this way your affirmation becomes a true statement that creates new energy and enthusiasm.

When we land our dream job, we will want a promotion, and eventually we will want a different job. When we find our ideal home, we will then want a bigger home. Again, we're always in process, so it's okay to say, "I'm in the process of (fill in the blank)."

Even though many affirmation experts believe your statements should always be in the present tense, such as, "I drive my favorite car," "I am thin," "I live in my dream home," there are times when you know that you don't have what you desire, nor do you *believe* you can have what you desire. As a result, it's hard to feel positive about an affirmation you know is not true.

Adding "I'm in the process of" (or one of the other "ing" suggestions listed) to the beginning of an affirmation helps your desire become more believable to you.

> **Key point:** The process of attracting what you want starts when you are focused on your desire and add lots of positive energy and enthusiasm.

You set energy in motion whenever you're thinking, talking, writing, and daydreaming about your desires. So when you say "I'm in the process of," that statement becomes true for you and feels good. You send positive vibes, which the Law of Attraction responds to by sending you more positive vibes.

Remember, we are always in the process of creation.

Exercise: Complete the sentence below in the space provided.

I am in the process of:

_____

_____

_____

_____

_____

_____

_____

Tool #7:

Tweak The Words Until They Feel Good

By now you understand that your thoughts, words, and emotions create the events in your life. Tweaking the words in your affirmation can make the difference between what works and what doesn't.

Here's one more suggestion to make you say, "Ah, now this feels really good." If doubt and resistance are still causing you to feel slightly uncomfortable, try including the word "ideal" in your affirmations.

Example: If my affirmation is to own an expensive, fancy sports car such as a BMW convertible, typically my affirmation would read: "I own a BMW convertible." But if I have limiting beliefs, I may feel bad saying I own something that I really cannot afford and will never be able to afford. My doubt creeps in when I look in the garage, see my old used car, and say, "Yeah right, who am I kidding?" Sadly, this is a common scenario, and people give up on this kind of affirmation in a week or even a day.

However, I could change the statement to: "My *ideal* car is a BMW convertible."

Inserting the word "ideal" fits the criteria of a positive affirmation because it lets me legitimately feel good about the fact that a BMW convertible is my ideal car. It doesn't matter whether I own it or not.

This phrasing is a little different than affirming that I drive a BMW convertible when I know I don't. It lessens my doubt and resistance. It allows me to state my desire in a truthful way. It allows me to feel good about my ideal car, dream about it, talk about it, and get excited about it. The Law of Attraction will respond to my positive vibration.

Exercise: Fill in the blanks below to discover how inserting "ideal" in your affirmations may feel good to you. Add other desires you may think of now that you have this positive tool.

My ideal relationship

_____

My ideal job

_____

My ideal customer

_____

My ideal health

_____

My ideal body

_____

My ideal vacation

_____

My ideal house

_____

My ideal car

_____

My ideal bank account

_____

My ideal

_____

My ideal

_____

My ideal

_____

Tool #8:

Kick Off Your Affirmations With Dynamic Language

You've now seen how you can use 7 new tools to reframe your affirmations so they are believable to you. Here are some additional "feel good" ways to kick off your positive statements.

- I feel safe knowing _____ .

- I appreciate _____ .

- I choose to _____ .

- I love knowing _____ .

- I enjoy _____ .

- It feels good to _____ .

- I love attracting _____ .

- Ideally _____ .

- I intend to _____ .

- It's great knowing that _____ .

- I'm committed to _____ .

- I deserve _____ .

- I am moving toward _____ .

- I am grateful for _____ .

- I've decided _____ .

Part IV:

Focus For Greater Results

You know that much of your success will come from your ability to focus your affirmations on specific goals.

Let's take the new tools you just learned and apply them to what you really want.

Exercise: On the next few pages, please do the following:

1. If your current affirmations are true for you and they feel good, write them on the following pages. Circle the plus sign for those that feel good and the minus sign for those that don't.
2. If you choose the minus sign for any affirmation that gives you a negative feeling, keep tweaking its wording, using the tools we've covered, until each feels good to you.
3. If you become stuck, you'll see samples below of "Success Affirmations" that you might use.

Key point: Remember this secret to making every affirmation work for you:
"If it feels good, use it. If it doesn't feel good, don't!"

Affirmations For Health

My Affirmations:

1. _____ Vibration + -

2. _____ Vibration + -

3. _____ Vibration + -

4. _____ Vibration + -

5. _____ Vibration + -

"*Dynamic Affirmation*" samples:

- I deeply and completely accept the way I feel today.

  Vibration + -

- I'm willing to begin to be more healthy.

  Vibration + -

- My body is producing new and healthy cells every day.

  Vibration + -

- I'm in the process of getting better each day.

  Vibration + -

- I'm willing to take steps for a healthier lifestyle.

  Vibration + -

- Every day I get better and better.   Vibration + -

- I take positive steps each day for healthful living.

  Vibration + -

- I'm eating healthfully and feeling the results every day.   Vibration + -

- I choose to feel _____

  Vibration + -

- I'm in the process of creating my ideal health.

  Vibration + -

- I appreciate _____

  Vibration + -

- Thank you for my healthy cells, and my beautiful _____ (hair, legs, eyes, etc.)   Vibration + -

Affirmations For Prosperity And Abundance

My Affirmations:

1. _____ Vibration + -

2. _____ Vibration + -

3. _____ Vibration + -

4. _____ Vibration + -

5. _____ Vibration + -

"Dynamic Affirmation" **samples:**

- I choose to attract a stronger positive vibration around money.   Vibration + -

- I expect to attract a better feeling about money.
  Vibration + -

- Making money energizes me.   Vibration + -

- Anything is possible.   Vibration + -

- There are many millionaires and I can be one too.
  Vibration + -

- I am worthy.   Vibration + -

- I already have enough money for all that I need.
                                             Vibration + -

- I choose to have an abundance of money.
                                             Vibration + -

- I love knowing I'm in the process of becoming
  financially independent.   Vibration + -

- Abundance is all around me.   Vibration + -

- There is more than enough for all.   Vibration + -

- I deserve prosperity.   Vibration + -

- Abundance is my birthright.   Vibration + -

- Thank you for the abundance in my life.
                                             Vibration + -

Affirmations For Success

My Affirmations:

1. _____ Vibration + -

2. _____ Vibration + -

3. _____ Vibration + -

4. _____ Vibration + -

5. _____ Vibration + -

"*Dynamic Affirmation*" samples:

* I am successful in all that I do. Vibration + -

* I easily and successfully achieve my goals.

  Vibration + -

* I am in the process of living my dreams.

  Vibration + -

* I am a powerful creator. Vibration + -

* I attract all the right resources to build my business.

  Vibration + -

- I am committed to growing my business.

    Vibration + -

- I have the talent necessary to have a successful career. Vibration + -

- If they can do it, so can I. Vibration + -

- Success is the sum of small efforts repeated daily.

    Vibration + -

- I can achieve anything I put my mind to.

    Vibration + -

- I am resourceful and always figure out a solution.

    Vibration + -

- I am focused and deserve success. Vibration + -

- I have complete control over how I spend my time.

    Vibration + -

- Thank you for the success in my life. Vibration + -

Affirmations For Overall Well-Being

My Affirmations:

1. _____ Vibration + -

2. _____ Vibration + -

3. _____ Vibration + -

4. _____ Vibration + -

5. _____ Vibration + -

"Dynamic Affirmation" samples:

- I feel happy and peaceful today.   Vibration + -

- I am learning to love myself more and more each day.   Vibration + -

- I love myself.   Vibration + -

- I deserve happiness.   Vibration + -

- I forgive myself.   Vibration + -

- I am worthy.   Vibration + -

- I'm completely satisfied and I want satisfaction to continue.   Vibration + -

- Everything is working for my highest good.
                                          Vibration + -

- The world is cooperating in my favor.   Vibration + -

- I deeply love, forgive, and accept myself.
                                          Vibration + -

- Out of this experience only good will come.
                                          Vibration + -

- Thank you for all the blessings I have.   Vibration + -

Affirmations For Love And Relationships

My Affirmations:

1. _____ Vibration + -

2. _____ Vibration + -

3. _____ Vibration + -

4. _____ Vibration + -

5. _____ Vibration + -

"Dynamic Affirmation" samples:

- Love comes to me easily and effortlessly.

  Vibration + -

- I give and receive love easily and joyfully.

  Vibration + -

- I express my love freely, knowing that as I give love I
  receive love.   Vibration + -

- I radiate love.   Vibration + -

- I allow people to love me.   Vibration + -

- I deserve love.   Vibration + -

- I am attracting loving relationships into my life.
                                                     Vibration + -

- I project love to everyone I meet.   Vibration + -

- I love and approve of myself.   Vibration + -

- My heart is open and receptive to giving and
  receiving love.   Vibration + -

- I am worthy of love.   Vibration + -

- I am now ready, willing, and able to allow love to
  flow into my life.   Vibration + -

- I attract healthy relationships.   Vibration + -

- I am love.   Vibration + -

Additional Affirmations

My Affirmations:

1. _____ Vibration + -

2. _____ Vibration + -

3. _____ Vibration + -

4. _____ Vibration + -

5. _____ Vibration + -

6. _____ Vibration + -

7. _____ Vibration + -

8. _____ Vibration + -

9. _____ Vibration + -

10. _____ Vibration + -

Part V:

Dynamic Tools
For Accelerated Results

*If all your affirmations feel really good,
let's speed up the process and
proactively tap into the
attraction effect for accelerated results.
The additional tools in this section help you do that.*

Tool #9:

Be Conscious Of What You Affirm

Example: If five times today you state a positive affirmation, but ten times today you doubt or talk about what you don't have (negative energy), you are cancelling out your positive affirmation.

Let's say you are affirming your prosperity, but throughout the day you look in your wallet and say, "I'm broke. I don't have any money!" Or, "I can't afford that." You are actually affirming poverty and wonder why money is not showing up.

> **Key point: Contradictory energies cancel out what you do want.**

Observing the negative stuff over and over can make you feel bad, and the situation just gets worse because you're in the vibration of "I'm broke."

You've poured your energy into creating and rewording your affirmations so they feel true and believable to you. Now make it a point to catch yourself--or to give others permission to catch you--whenever you state what you don't want or have. In time you will be talking more and more about what you *do* want, and each positive statement will naturally become a consistent thought process.

Exercise: List two affirmations and what you might be saying or doing to cancel out each one.

1. Positive Affirmation:

_____

a. Conflicting Negative Statement:

_____

b. Conflicting Negative Statement:

_____

_____

2. Positive Affirmation:

_____

a. Conflicting Negative Statement:

_____

b. Conflicting Negative Statement:

_____

Tool #10:

Intentionally Focus On Your Affirmations

> *"Constant repetition carries conviction.*
> *Repeat your affirmations often.*
> *Write them down and constantly remind yourself of them.*
> *Let them be branded in your mind so you are constantly*
> *thinking of or referring to them."*
> – Robert Collier

Example: Select one or two affirmations to really give your attention and lots of energy to. The Law of Attraction can bring what you desire, but you must be clear about what you want and give it your attention and energy.

We typically think of standing in front of the mirror repeating affirmations, and if that works for you keep doing so.

There are lots of other ways you can keep your affirmations at the forefront of your mind. Examples include:

- Creating and tweaking your affirmation means you are focusing on what you want and raising your vibration.

- Read each affirmation out loud with enthusiasm.

- Memorize each and repeat them throughout the day.

- Talk about them with your friends and family.

- Sing your affirmations.

- Print your affirmations and place them in a picture frame.

- Visualize the reality that the words embrace.

- Journal about each affirmation.

- Ask yourself "why" you want your desire which allows you to get excited about it.

- Write your affirmations over and over.

- Daydream about them.

- Create a story around each affirmation and think of all the wonderful possibilities for each.

- Repeat each one just prior to meditating or going to sleep. (Your sub-conscious mind will go to work to bring what you desire without resistance from your conscious mind).

- Create a Vision Board by going through the process of cutting out pictures of what you want and placing them on a board to hang on your wall.

Keep in mind that whichever of these suggestions feels good, do it. If any doesn't feel good, don't do it.

Key point: Most importantly, *feel* your positive affirmations.

Why? Because that's what the Law of Attraction responds to.

Exercise: List some additional ways you can focus on your affirmations.

1. _____

   _____

2. _____

   _____

3. _____

   _____

4. _____

   _____

5. _____

   _____

Tool #11:
You Gotta Feeeeel The Vibrational Resonance

Affirmations work when they are in vibrational resonance with your desires.

Example: Your emotions are your only way to gauge whether you are attracting what you want. When you feel good you are attracting what you want; when you feel bad it's your indication you are attracting what you don't want.

Energy attracts like energy. You are like a human magnet. Therefore, to attract your desire it makes sense that you be in vibrational resonance with--or a vibrational match to--what you desire.

When you want abundance, you must be in the energy of abundance. For instance, feeling either the need for money or the lack of money keeps you from experiencing the vibration of money. It won't show up. Prosperity is a different vibration from poverty.

If you feel poor you can't become prosperous. You must *feel* prosperous.

You can't attract good health if you *feel* unhealthy.

You can't attract love if you *feel* unlovable.

You can't attract success if you *feel* undeserving.

Key point: If you are *feeling* lack in any area, you can only attract more lack.

You must send the vibration that matches your desire, not the vibration of what you currently have.

The matching of vibes to desires is why it's so important that you pay attention to the way you feel. Whether or not you already have your desire or seem likely to reach your desire, you can nevertheless find a way to feel good about it.

Test drive that new car, go house hunting, pick up travel brochures and talk about your favorite destinations. Daydream about your desire so having it feels good and you become in vibrational resonance with it. The secret is to assume the *feeling* of what you want and find ways to maintain that vibration!

Exercise: Use the space below to answer the question, "What can I do to get in vibrational resonance with what I want?"

1. _____

2. _____

3. _____

4. _____

5. _____

6. _____

7. _____

8. _____

9. _____

10. _____

Tool #12:

Discover Endless Possibilities With The Abundance Game

Often we try to figure out where our desire & goal can come from. When we do this, we close our mind to the endless possibilities and opportunities available to us.

Example: Have you ever been in need of money, figured it could come only from your paycheck, and out of the blue an unexpected check arrived in the mail? You never would have guessed you'd get a check from this source. Or maybe you were expecting a job offer from a particular company and another position just opened up, one that was more in alignment with what you really wanted.

The abundance game allows you to brainstorm by yourself or with others the unlimited possibilities of how your desire can come to you. Brainstorming implies that you speak or write anything that comes to mind. No second guessing, no evaluating, judging, or filtering of information based on thinking it may not work--just keep going until you exhaust all ideas.

When you open yourself up to all of the possibilities, you get excited, you see that what you want can come from anywhere, and you experience the *feeling* of what you desire. These are the behaviors that place you in vibrational resonance with your desire.

Here are two ways to use the abundance game to attract what you want.

1. *How many ways can I attract great health?* I can take a class in healthful cooking, join the gym, take up yoga, learn meditation, talk about the healthy parts of me and what I love about myself (e.g., my eyes, legs, nose), find a positive support group, read books that are motivational and inspiring, be mindful of the types of relationships I keep, be conscious and cautious of the words I use and thoughts I think, and so much more!

2. *How many ways can I attract my ideal partner?* At work, the gym, volunteering, PTA meetings, business trips, dating service, sporting events, Little League games, neighborhood gatherings, and networking functions.

You get the idea. Open your mind to all the possibilities rather than to what won't work.

Exercise: Make a list of the many ways you can attract what you want. Whatever comes to mind, jot it down.

1. _____

2. _____

3. _____

4. _____

5. _____

6. _____

7. _____

8. _____

9. _____

10. _____

Tool #13:

Create Your Mini-Movie To Speed The Process

For best results, dedicate some time for this exercise upon waking in the morning and before drifting off to sleep at night. No time in the morning? That's okay. Do this exercise whenever and wherever you get the opportunity.

Example: Following are some ways to engage all five of your senses to speed up the process of making your affirmations come true. This exercise allows you to create a mini-movie about your desires. It triggers all of your emotions and is one of the fastest ways to achieve vibrational resonance with what you desire.

Close your eyes and run your mini-movie in your head. Not only does it feel good to star in your own movie, but when you play your movie without criticism or resistance, you are setting the energy in motion to bring you your desire.

Here's how to direct your mini-movie:

- See yourself having accomplished your goal. What does it look like? What are you doing?

- Rehearse what you will say to yourself or to others. Hear your words.

- Feel the emotion of success.

- Sense how your body feels.

- Smell whatever aromas might be connected to this success.

- Taste whatever flavors may be connected to this success.

- Combine all these and visualize yourself having attained your goal.

- Put yourself into this movie as an active participant and absorb all of the wonderful feelings.

Key point: When you use all of your senses to flow strong positive energy toward your desire, the closer you'll come to realize your dreams.

Example: Let's say you want to live near the ocean. You might create this affirmation: "I am in the process of living near the ocean." Create a mini-movie and run it once every morning and every evening. Close your eyes. Take a deep breath. Watch the waves as they gently roll onto the shore. Hear the cry of the seagulls. Feel the delicate breeze on your face and flowing through your hair. Can you smell the salt in the air? What words might you say? Dig your toes into the sand and notice whether it is hot or cool. Is the sun rising or setting? Walk along the shore rather than just picturing yourself walking along the shore. Be it, feel it. Remember the Law of Attraction responds to the *feeling*.

Exercise: In the space below, write your mini-movie involving all your senses and really, really, feel it!

_____

_____

_____

_____

_____

_____

_____

_____

_____

_____

Tool #14:

Use Emotional Anchors

Here's a quick little tool that helps put you in the *feeling* place that the Law of Attraction responds to.

Example: Recall a wonderful memory that is in line with the affirmation you want to attract. For instance, if you want to attract success, think of a time when you *felt* successful. If you want to attract your ideal relationship, recall a memory when you *felt* really loved.

Recalling that wonderful memory does two things:

1. It puts you in the feeling place where you can send positive vibes that the Law of Attraction (which is always checking) will respond to.

2. While you are re-experiencing that powerful memory, use all of your senses as if you were there again. Evoke all the emotions associated with that memory. Then, state your new affirmation and repeat it. These inspired actions link your new affirmation with the powerful feelings that already exist from your wonderful memory.

The process binds your new affirmation to your subconscious mind far more powerfully.

Exercise: List memories that evoke a flood of positive emotions.

1. _____

2. _____

3. _____

4. _____

5. _____

6. _____

7. _____

8. _____

9. _____

10. _____

Once you're fully experiencing the feeling of your wonderful memory, introduce your new affirmation and ride that high vibration for as long as you can. I recommend doing this exercise several times throughout your day. It's quick, it's easy, and fun!

Tool #15:

Give Appreciation And Gratitude

Example: Appreciation and gratitude represent one of the highest forms of vibrations we can send. When we're experiencing a *feeling* of appreciation and gratitude, we're in vibrational resonance with it, and the Law of Attraction gives us more to be thankful for.

Recalling, writing, and telling friends what we're grateful for are behaviors that make up the fastest way to shift your feelings from sad, angry, worried, and depressed to a higher value of vibration.

Even if you may not feel abundant right now, you can nevertheless think of some things you can feel grateful for--perhaps your family, relationships, food, good health, a car that runs, a comfortable bed. You might appreciate a beautiful sunrise, a colorful garden, or a friendly smile from a stranger!

Make a deliberate point to focus on something and flood it with appreciation until you feel the vibration change. Once you feel it change, stay in that energy for as long as you can. You will open yourself up to receiving wonderful results.

Key point: Make the deliberate choice to *feel* appreciation and gratitude to get into vibrational resonance with it. You'll *feel* great!

Exercise: Write down everything you feel grateful for today.

1. _____

2. _____

3. _____

4. _____

5. _____

6. _____

7. _____

8. _____

9. _____

10. _____

Daily Exercise:

Make it a practice to list ten or more things that you appreciate or feel grateful for immediately upon waking. Remember to really let the energy flow. You can't feel grateful and feel bad at the same time. You can have only one vibe at a time, positive or negative. Imagine carrying those great vibes with you throughout your day.

Tool #16:

Let Go Of Your Attachment To The Outcome

Become an observer, but don't judge the process. Trust and have faith that it's working.

If you have created your affirmations so they are true for you and feel good, your next step is to focus on them, add strong positive emotion by applying the tools provided in this chapter, then release the "HOW" by which you will get your desire.

Your job is not to manage the process but to trust the attraction effect and have faith that the Law of Attraction will bring the desired results to you. Trust takes emotional discipline. When you notice that a result has not yet shown up and you struggle, worry, and try to figure out a way, you are sending a negative vibration and actually resisting and pushing your desire away.

When you plant a seed in your garden, you water it and wait for it to bloom. You don't rip it out of the ground after one week and say this doesn't work.

If you find yourself trying to figure out why a result is taking more time than you thought it might, take responsibility for your thought and make the conscious choice to shift your attention to thoughts of a better feeling. Take a deep breath, relax, affirm your positive statement, and do something that brings you joy. Trust that you are applying the proven, successful tools in this book and setting your positive energy in motion. That's your job. The Law of Attraction will do its job--which is to match the vibration that you're sending.

Exercise: Ask yourself the following questions and write your responses below.

1. How have I been managing the process?

_____

_____

_____

_____

2. What strategies will I use to take my attention away from managing the process?

_____

_____

_____

_____

Tool #17:
Take Inspired Action

Affirmations alone do not cause results to happen in your life.

Example: When Napoleon Hill wrote *Think and Grow Rich*, he didn't mean that all you had to do was to think about what you wanted and it would magically appear.

> **Key point: Thinking about a desire is just the beginning. There is also action you must take.**

What is the appropriate action to take?
As humans, we're conditioned to take action. We like to fix things and make them better. We often struggle and force things to work out. But we're not talking about taking action solely for the sake of taking action and forcing our affirmations and goals to work.

Action without inspiration is dis-connected energy!
When you create *Dynamic Affirmations* that feel good and get into vibrational resonance with them, you will be

inspired to take action. The ideas and information come to you, the situations appear, and everything flows easily.

If you don't know the next step to take, just take the step that seems most logical to you and open yourself to receiving more inspired action. If you keep moving forward, you're going to get there, even if it means taking baby steps.

When the time is right, new opportunities do line up to make action happen.

Key point: It's the flowing of inspired energy that brings you what you want.

If your action feels like work, if you feel as if you're hitting your head against a brick wall, you're not in the flow of pure positive energy.

1. Revisit your affirmation to make sure it feels good and is believable to you.

2. Use the tools provided in this book to get into vibrational harmony with your affirmation.

3. You will naturally feel inspired to take the next step. You'll know when the timing is right and what the correct step to take is by the way you feel. Be sure to act on those hunches and nudges! They are your signal that everything is lining up in your favor.

Exercise: Ask yourself the following questions:

Am I forcing circumstances to occur in my life? _____

What actions have I taken toward my affirmations or goals that seemed difficult?

1. _____

2. _____

3. _____

4. _____

5. _____

If you've been following along with each tool thus far, you may already feel inspired to take action. Name the next logical step or series of steps you can take toward attracting one of your affirmations to you.

1. _____

2. _____

3. _____

4. _____

5. _____

PART VI:

Bonus Chapter:
Tools Applied by Real People

Throughout history people from all walks of life have created affirmations or positive statements, stated intentions, repeated mantras, or set goals to attract what they want. Some enjoyed enormous success while others gave up. You learned from *Dynamic Affirmations* why this is so.

Affirmations are not created equal. We want the little box of affirmation cards available at the bookstore to apply to all people and all situations. But that's just not the case.

What works for one person doesn't necessarily work for another. That's why Jodi sat down with a number of successful individuals and interviewed them to find out which tool or tools worked best for each of them in creating their affirmations and getting real results.

Jodi shares those many tools with you in this book. You have only to accept the process of discovering which tools resonate most with you, then commit to using them.

Please visit www.CreateAffirmations.com for additional interviews and to download audio interviews.

A World Champion Speaker's Perspective:

Darren LaCroix

My Background

In 2001 after winning the title of World Champion of Public Speaking, I quit my day job even though I was barely earning enough to pay my bills. So each morning I wrote, "I earn $500,000 per year in my speaking business." I filled a sheet of lined paper every morning with that affirmation. I had some modest success but I never came close to earning that figure. Quite frankly I stopped using the affirmation after months and months. Doubts led to more thoughts of doubt.

I think the affirmation made me feel like a liar. It also focused on money, and though I wanted to earn more, for me money should not be the focus. **I think we have to know who we are and be congruous with our beliefs of who we want to be.** Being brought up Roman Catholic, I have some deep-seated beliefs, many of which serve me well and keep me doing the "right" thing. I'm not passing judgment on anyone else, nor am I saying all of my beliefs serve me, but while reading the book *Secrets of the Millionaire Mind,* I discovered a belief I had created as a child that was incorrect, and was holding me back from believing I deserved to earn more. I could do all the affirmations I wanted, but unless they got me past that one, I wasn't going to be changing my income level any time soon-or maybe ever.

For me, I needed to **tweak my affirmations** to serve others, thus making the income a byproduct. For example, **"I inspire so many people through my speaking and educational tools that I earn $500,000 per year."**

My Affirmation Story

When I entered the Toastmasters International World Championship of Public Speaking--a speech contest in which over 25,000 contestants compete from more than 14 countries--my goal was not to win but to become a better speaker. My professional speaking career had been growing slowly, with no signs of huge success on the horizon. My mentors had taught me that becoming professional was not about being the best at writing new speeches. It was about being so good at telling your stories that people were willing to pay to hear them. I had it wrong, but I am coachable.

I saw the contest as a tool to force me to work on the stories I was already telling as a keynote speaker. If I improved the best parts of my speech, I would improve the value of the whole speech. This would increase my referral rate every time I spoke. When you have no advertising budget, this plan makes perfect sense.

I selected my best story, the inspiring story of my first time on stage at a comedy open mic night. It won me the first four levels of the contest. At the fifth level, everyone is required to write a new speech. Judges have an outline from the previous contest level in front of them to make sure the contestant changes the speech. I did, and I won. For the next level, again I had to write a new speech, and I had seventy-seven days to write it from scratch. I had never before started from a blank piece of paper but used stories I had already been telling. This was a huge problem for me because I had already used my best stories.

I had heard about affirmations and was very skeptical of them. I felt affirmations and visualizations were a load of empty "happy thoughts" that I didn't really believe could work. But I thought what if they did work? Though I might feel like a dork I figured no one would see me doing them.

Every day I got up and ran four miles to help my body deal with the stress and the emotional highs and lows along the way. People in my district rallied around me to set up all 22 speeches that I gave. They also gathered 10 years of World Championship videos from past winners for me to study. I met Mark Brown, the 1995 World Champion of Public Speaking, who became my coach, and twice that summer I drove two and a half hours each way to work face-to-face with him. The feedback and the process of "questioning myself" became overwhelming at times. Because of the brutal feedback I received, which I needed, three times that summer when I went to sleep I was ready to quit. Three times my subconscious solved the problem I had with my speech and I woke up with the answers.

My Affirmation Tools

In *Toastmaster Magazine* I saw a picture of the previous winner holding the trophy above his head with two hands. I decided I would use that photo and visualize my holding the trophy in the air, but with one hand. I also decided to fill a sheet of lined paper every morning with this statement: "I am the 2001 World Champion of Public Speaking."

Key point

Now that I've been studying the subconscious brain, I believe I understand much better why my affirmation worked for me. I believe saying and writing it out each morning helped attract the people and the circumstances I needed in order to win.

Darren LaCroix is a keynote speaker, author, speaker coach and the 2001 World Champion of Public Speaking. He can be reached at DarrenLaCroix.com.

Using Visualization Techniques For Weight And Body Image:

Eddie Hassell

My Background

I'm the kind of person who never knew much about affirmations as I was growing up. It wasn't part of my life. But I was seeing a therapist to help me with some issues, including body image, and she suggested something that had worked for her around overeating, which was to create an affirmation, stand in front of the mirror, look yourself in the eye, and with great conviction state that affirmation. So I created an affirmation to the effect of, "I am slender, I eat right, and I exercise." I stood in front of the mirror and said those words, and right away I knew they did not resonate with me. Within a day, I quit.

I used to look at physical exercise and think, "Okay, tomorrow morning I'm going to get out there and start running." Or "All right, I'm going to hit that weight room . . . starting Monday." Over a bowl of ice cream I'd tell myself, "All right, it's exercise time tomorrow, buddy." But then I wouldn't get up in the morning, or I'd let myself down. I didn't do what I'd told myself I would.

My Affirmation Story

I was invited to a four-day silent retreat. I went to the retreat and for four days stayed in silence. I decided to use the quiet space offered to me to create visions of what I wanted my life to be, so I picked four areas I wanted to work on. I've already talked about my body and weight, but I also added spirituality, job and career, and relationships.

What happened is that I kind of introduced myself to the concept of baby steps, to **bringing things into my life in small increments** so that I could actually enjoy them. Or I enjoy them because they are small increments. Now I say to myself, "You can walk 20 minutes a day in the morning."

I have my little routine where I do the meditation/visualization work, then I take a walk for 20 minutes on the treadmill or outside, and I go to yoga. I've introduced yoga into my life several times a week, and all these things are now enjoyable. They're not work anymore, so I do them. **I was inspired to action. The action is in small steps, and the small steps are enjoyable, from which I get good feelings. So I then step up to another level where I incorporate something else that's enjoyable and gives me a good feeling, and that steps me up a little more. It's like an upward spiral**--slow, but enjoyable.

My Affirmation Tools

My inspired action was to spend 20 minutes every morning--sometimes an hour--in quiet reflection in a workshop in my head. I tried meditation, but meditation wasn't working for me consistently. Instead, I go to my little **visualization workshop** and I tinker with the visions. More importantly, now that the visions have begun to get clear and crystallize, I try to **feel that vision**, to get in that place of actually experiencing what a good job feels like, what a good relationship feels like.

I call myself a data collector and that data collecting is an important component of this reflection time. As I go through my day, I collect images of little things I see that I like. I see them and I bring them in to my visualizations, and I remember how I felt about each when I saw it. So I spend time in that feeling as often as I can. An example of what I mean by data collection occurs with a woman at work who thinks I'm really funny. Our sense of humor is exactly the same. I'll say something, and before anyone else can catch on, she cracks up, even in the middle of a meeting! She'll say, "Eddie, you are so funny!" She's a married woman and there's no intent on my part to create a relationship with her, but I take away the feeling she gives me by enjoying my humor. I incorporate that feeling in my workshop and carry it around with me. I remind myself, "How do you feel when she does that? It feels good. Okay, then feel that." Data collection, visualization--they create a nice clear view of what it is I want.

One has to be willing to view this whole experience as a journey, one that has no destination but is actually fun to be in the process. To be thinking this way is fun, like being at the top of a roller coaster. Some days I get plenty of what I call "contrast," remembering the way I used to think or about what it is I DON'T want. I see it very clearly and now I can look at it and say, "I don't want to think like that." The contrast is important, it offers the opportunity to remember what it is I DO want.

Here's an affirmation I use now: **"I am moving toward a healthy body. I am aware that every cell in my body seeks balance and can repair itself. Every cell in my body is connected to the universal wellness. I trust my body to do the right thing. I am becoming more aware of my body and its signals. As I eat now, I am eating more consciously and paying more attention to the signal that I am full. I am becoming more aware of the signals about what to eat as well as how much to eat. I am moving toward a healthy holistic relationship with food. I am loving my exercise program and I get more comfortable in my own skin every day."**

I know now that I'm capable of having a healthy, beautiful relationship; I can have the perfect job for me; I can provide relief for others; I can go through my day and not let anyone get me in a bad mood for a whole day.

Whatever words you use, it's your story. As you look out you should revise and improve that vision, then look at that. Don't look at things that are haunting you or that are not good for you or do things you don't want. **Look only at this improved story.**

Key point

All improvement is a process, and enjoying the process is important. As I move toward the manifestation of my weight goal, I have incorporated exercise into my life and a change in my eating habits. Most importantly, I came to **accept myself the way I am**, a huge step for me. I recommend revising and improving the content of your own story each and every day.

To get to know Eddie better, visit him via Facebook (facebook. com) under his name, "Eddie Hassell."

Motivational Speaker And Writer Uses Affirmations To Enhance All Aspects Of Her Life:

Angie Bowker

My Background

In three and a half years I went from being a 21-year employee, the mother of a son very active in sports, and in a relationship moving toward marriage, to all of that changing: the loss of my job through a cutback, my son's two heart procedures, and the end of my relationship. I looked at all the goals I'd been working toward and said, "Wow, none of these work for me anymore." I had to step back and say, "Okay, I guess I have to have some new goals and some new dreams."

My introduction to affirmations--or positive thinking, positive statements and goals--is much like that of many people, wanting to have a change in life, going to the local bookstore or getting online and looking for resources. Pretty much anything I came across referred me back to some type of affirmation or the word "goals." Today I'd be able to say something positive about each event. Then, to say I had a strategy with very specific, focused affirmations to reach my goals--I look back and see I didn't have that.

My Affirmation Story

I was at a business event doing an exercise known as "clarity through contrast" relating to my job, and all of a sudden I had a vision of what my career needed to look like. I realized that where I was at the time did not fit that picture, and it got me focusing on affirmations and going back to the heart of the matter. First I developed a very simple affirmation: **"I am bold and powerful."** That empowered me to start taking steps forward in the things I wanted to achieve, because I now had clarity about what I wanted my career to look like.

I can say an affirmation all day long, but if there isn't some action put forth to support it, the affirmation doesn't have the power it needs to move me forward. So when I saw an opportunity to be bold, I was bold. For something I feel passionate about, I focused on the word "powerful," and when I had an opportunity to be bold in a position of power, I took the opportunity to help move something forward. Like draws like, and that's exactly what started happening in my life.

The other affirmation I regularly say is **"I am beautiful."** When I look in the mirror and say "I am beautiful," that promotes action. It makes me want to go to the gym, treat myself to a nice haircut and occasionally to a new item of clothing. All these things tie in to making me feel better, which gets me striving toward health indirectly instead of focusing on health to start with.

When someone goes through a lot of life changes it's hard to say your life is wonderful. I decided I wanted my life to be wonderful, so a third affirmation was to say, **"My life is wonderful."**

Everybody has financial concerns, so a fourth affirmation was, **"My finances and wisdom are increasing."** I knew I wasn't there yet, and if I created an affirmation as if I'd already attained that, subconsciously I'd know I was lying to myself. I knew I needed to phrase the one on finance correctly so I could believe that my wisdom and my finances were increasing.

My Affirmation Tools

Once I realized how to develop my affirmations, I did an inventory of every area of my life. I got a new journal, and at the top of a page wrote the year followed by: "is My Year to Shine." I listed the different areas of my life, then asked, "Am I happy and content in these areas?" I contrasted the things I didn't like about each with what I did want each to look like.

Then I honed the list so I wouldn't have 25 affirmations but four or five that would apply to the key areas of my life I wanted to focus on. That worked for me.

I carry my journal with me so I look at those affirmations each morning and many times throughout the day. If I'm in a situation and sense negative feelings starting, I immediately stop and say all five of my affirmations, one after the other, which kind of flips a switch in my brain to push the negative thoughts out. I've learned those are the critical times I must stop and repeat an affirmation as if it's automatic. Doing so becomes as simple as breathing. I had to start looking at things through a positive lens instead of a negative lens.

Key point

You have first got to be real with yourself about what you like and don't like, and want for yourself, your career, and your life. Only when you're real with yourself can you start creating affirmations you can truly hold on to and believe are true for you.

Angie is a certified realtor, consultant, motivational speaker, and author of the upcoming Christian children's book series "Secret Mission Series." She can be found on both Facebook (www.facebook.com) and Twitter (www.twitter.com) under her name, Angie Bowker.

Speaker And Consultant Uses Affirmations To Achieve His Business Goals:

Mark Green

My Background

I moved through adolescence and into my professional life with some disdain for the concept of affirmations. For that I can thank Jack Handy from *Saturday Night Live*. His skits used to have affirmations such as "I love myself" and "I'm a wonderful person," which convinced me that affirmations were not for me, because I didn't need those kinds of things. I couldn't see any connection between the concept of affirmations as I knew it from tv and applying it to move myself forward.

I started hearing from my colleagues about affirmations and how they are very effective. So I started recommending to some clients that they begin using focused affirmations. For my own integrity I couldn't just tell my clients, "Hey, this affirmation stuff is great; you have to use it," without also using it myself. So I started by creating some fairly straightforward, focused statements for myself that at the time were most relevant to me. What's interesting is that they're still very relevant to me.

My Affirmations Story

One of the problems I had early in my consulting practice, particularly when I was in sales mode, was my tendency to talk too much, so I created a simple affirmation: **"I ask more than I tell."** It's been a powerful one for me. I use it at times as a reminder, such as when I'm about to get out of my car for an appointment. It keeps me focused in the most productive way I can be in that moment.

For me to grow my business and have the success I want to have, I need to become known as somebody who has influence. So the affirmation I created is: "**I always do what I say I will do.**" That keeps me from putting myself in a situation where I've overcommitted and under-delivered. It forces me to a standard that I believe is the right standard for me.

Another affirmation of mine is, **"My yes means yes and my no means no."** It helps keep me focused. It means I need to make a decision and I need to move.

My final affirmation is, **"I am open to receive."** This helps put me in a place where I start to expect that good things are going to happen. It's not specific only to the business or to winning a new client or that kind of thing. It's being open to anything--in relationships, in networking, anything, anywhere. Being open to receiving helps me stay focused on that part of me needing to be ready for the good stuff coming my way.

My Affirmation Tools

The first thing to have is goals. If I don't have clear goals for myself or for whatever business endeavor I'm pursuing, I'm going to have a very hard time creating affirmations, because **affirmations need to be directional, aligned with goals in the first-person singular and in the present tense.**

Second, **affirmations need to be specific.** If I aspire to be a millionaire and I create an affirmation that says, "I am a millionaire," how does that help me connect with the behaviors of a millionaire? It doesn't. To have, I must first become. To have a million dollars, I must first become the kind of person who's worth a million dollars. All of my affirmations concern my behavior and my thinking.

For some people, three affirmations are plenty. A list of 10, 15, or 20 affirmation statements lacks focus. The process I use, the process I instruct my clients to use, is the process I've witnessed gets results. I **pick three or four affirmations**--not a different three or four every day. I write all three on each of three index cards and put one card where I see it when I get up in the morning, one where I see it before I go to bed at night, and one where I see it around the middle of the day. I hold the card in my hand and read each affirmation statement out loud three times.

I urge others to give this method a try and **make a commitment to yourself to do it for 30 days**, because anything less than 30 doesn't give you a real chance to benefit. If after 30 days the process doesn't work for you, then you can say it doesn't work for you--which would astound me, by the way, because what most people see after 30 days is that the power is absolutely incredible.

Key point

The most powerful tool is the process. The process is ultimately what's going to lead to the result much more than any phrase written on a piece of paper. Give yourself a chance and make it work.

Mark Green is a developer of business affirmation tools called "Mind Clings"™ (MindClings.com). He also has a consulting company, Performance Dynamics Group, and can be found at MarkGreenSpeaks.com. He consults for small and mid-sized companies, helping them find how to become more proactive and less reactive.

Using Vision Boards And Meditation To Attract What's Wanted:

Mariellen Mclean

My Background

I didn't grow up using affirmations but I did read quotes that my father had posted on his office wall, inspirational sayings such as, **"It's not the mountains ahead that wear you down, it's the grain of sand in your shoes,"** which means that many things are possible if you aren't bogged down with the small stuff. Don't spend your energy on insignificant events such as someone cutting you off in traffic, or because your boss is being mean to you. Don't let those small things hold you back from climbing your mountain.

My reason for not using affirmations is that many times they didn't feel authentic. I felt I was saying something that was not real. For instance, I was in a job that was very unhealthy for me. What I was doing didn't feel right. I'm in a helping profession, and at that point I felt as if I was hindering more people than I was helping, so I was really struggling. I didn't know what to do because it was a lucrative job, the money was good, and it had great benefits, but it just wasn't purposeful any more.

My Affirmation Story

I found myself at a networking meeting not being able to focus as I was thinking about these career issues, and I realized, "I have got to do something. I cannot continue. This just doesn't feel good." I had my Day-Timer with me, so at that moment I wrote an affirmation: **"Please direct me today toward people and opportunities that allow me to work with individuals of love and integrity, while I use my talents and skills to help and guide others, all the while loving what I do and having financial abundance."**

I picked an intention that is doable--something I can do that fulfills all the things I want to see happen in my life. I made the affirmation in a general language that was believable to me.   If I'd been too specific and said, "Please direct me to the Anderson Clinic; this is where I want to work," that might not be possible because it's too narrow a goal. Instead, what I wrote gave me a lot of possibilities in making it happen in different ways.

I read my affirmation for the first couple of weeks, and then forgot about it. A month or so ago I found it again, and I feel as if I am going through the process of that affirmation right now. I am no longer working in a stressful dysfunctional environment. I am in the process of enhancing my skills so that I can have a career with purpose. I am on my way! I know subconsciously the message has been there even though I hadn't been consciously reading it every day. Since I found it, I've put it on my board.

My Affirmation Tools

About 12 years ago I was working with geripsych patients in a partial hospital program, and we created "Wish" boards as part of their therapy. We'd get magazines and spend an afternoon cutting out pictures of what the patients wanted to have happen in their lives. It was a therapeutic exercise to help them to see the possibilities of the future beginning in the here and now. I've always done that for myself, too. I've done a board every two or three years, and it seems that when I have them where I can read them--whether in my office or in my bathroom at home--the things on my board do appear and they do happen.

My process in making my board usually takes a couple of weeks, or it may be continuous, kind of like an evolution. Some of the things on my vision board have come to pass--like my schnauzer. I'd been wishing for a little black schnauzer and I found Jax. His picture stayed on the board for a couple of months, to remind me that this really does work. Success doesn't happen in just one day; it happens when we consciously decide to bring into action what has come to mind. It's a development. Often I'll put quotes on my board such as "explore," "dream," "imagine," "hope," "love," "be impeccable with your words," and so on to help manifest my intentions.

Thanks to the Law of Attraction, I have my wonderful husband. I sat down and made a list of what I wanted in a partner, and honestly, everything I wrote down is present in this person--so the method does work. It's happened with my jobs, my dog, and my house. I put pictures of the house I wanted on my board and just recently moved into one that is very similar. The method works! My vision boards and the Law of Attraction just seem to work for me--and they always have.

I believing in asking yourself **what are you most passionate about? What brings you joy**? What is it you want to do and what natural talents can you enhance that will get you to your goals? Also think of what in your life you wanted to do but for some reason stopped you because you didn't think you were talented enough or didn't have the tools or didn't know the right people. First think about what it is you love to do. Get out of yourself and be around people and places that support that desire. Take Action!

I've found it helpful to read books by people who are on the same journey I'm on. I also meditate and kind of go within myself to find answers that are within. I've been amazed at what comes from that--maybe not immediately during the minutes I am meditating, but later. Meditation clears the clutter for me, and for some reason acts like a compass, pointing me in the right direction so I remember what my purposeful goal is. I enjoy doing yoga, too. It puts my mind in a creative and open mode. I suggest spending 5 to 10 minutes a day thinking about what you want to bring into your life. Talk with others about what you're doing, and listen for the ideas and suggestions of people who have good judgment.

Key point

I had to find a way to make my affirmations believable so I'd know it was possible and I could get where I wanted to be--unlike reading a statement that I believed was probably not going to happen no matter how many times I'd say it. Using sentences such as "I am in the process of," or "I am working toward," (whatever your goal is) will help you feel more authentic rather than using sentences that declare you have already achieved your desired outcome.

Mariellen has a Master's degree in Counseling Psychology and is currently working to get her LPC (Licensed Professional Counselor). She can be found on Facebook (facebook.com) under her name, "Mariellen McLean."

An Entrepreneur's Perspective
Successful Network Marketer Uses
Affirmations With Visualization:

Herman Luette

My Background

About 20, 25 years ago I was listening to an audiotape on goal setting. The speaker said if you want to reach your goals, you need to have positive affirmations. I didn't understand what that was, but the speaker used some examples. So I took my goals and phrased them into some positive affirmations based on what I was hearing on the audiotape.

I first started using my affirmations when I was in karate. Back in the eighties I was competing on the national karate circuit and I kept saying, "I am the national karate champion" and "I am the world heavyweight karate champion." I kept saying those statements, and because the audiotape speaker had said if you really want to achieve your goal use some visualization with it, I did. I started visualizing myself on the stage, receiving my trophy as the United States National Fighting Champion, then the World Heavyweight Fighting

Champion, then becoming part of the Hall of Fame. I kept picturing myself and saying each affirmation as if those goals were already happening. I believe the world gives you what you need, so sure enough my mind and the world gave me what I needed to actually reach my goals, every one of them. Today I continue to use different affirmations and visual techniques.

My Affirmation Story

I wanted to be the U.S. National Fighting Champion, so instead of just writing those words **I wrote them as if the reality had already happened**: "I am_____." Instead of saying "wanting to be" I said "I am"--and that's what gave me the extra edge, because the mind doesn't know that I haven't already done so. What I found out is that telling my mind that I'd already reached my goal, my mind gave me all the resources I needed to achieve that goal. In stating my affirmation, I tried to **feel the emotion**, the elation I'd experience by winning, hearing the audience clapping, putting myself right into that picture. Even though my body wasn't at the award ceremony, in my mind I was. Not only was the affirmation auditory as I was saying it, but also it was visual as my mind's eye saw my success. And I was feeling it, experiencing what it would feel like to actually achieve whatever goal I was working toward at the time. I believe one of the reasons I was able to attract my goal is that I was using all my senses to really experience each goal.

My Affirmation Tools

I'd always heard of writing down your goals. That's a big help for me. Putting my goals in front of me helps keep me motivated and on track. Every day, looking at my written goals reminds me that these are my goals, and that if I haven't reached them yet I'm still striving for them. Also it helps to have pictures of the things I'm going to achieve. If you have a particular house you want to get, a particular car you want, and maybe financial freedom, define these, especially financial freedom because it's very vague. I believe in being very definite about what I want. On my wall I have a commission check for one million dollars. I look at it and know I will reach that one-million-dollar goal with my company and become a millionaire. That's one of the ways I make my goals real.

What's worked for me is deciding what it is I want to achieve; the end result. If it's a million dollars, if it's recognition, if it's a house, if it's a car--whatever it is, I work back from the goal to figure out how I'm going to get it. I wanted a million dollars, so I wrote, **"I want to earn a million dollars."** Then I put the goal into an affirmation as if it already happened: "I am a millionaire in my company." I actually wrote a check, printed it out so it looks official, and put it up on my dream board. Then I wrote the activities on a dry-erase board that would help me achieve what I wanted.

I have several pictures posted on my dream board. I not only can read my goals but actually see them. If I read them and see them, I can get into the state of mind I need to be in if I'm to take action to achieve them. All these things are mounted on one wall, and all my pictures are framed so they are professional looking. They're not hung haphazardly but are framed around a dry-erase board. I use the board to write the activities that help me reach my goals and meet my affirmations. I use all of these together: my goals are written, my pictures are framed and hung, and the actions I'll take are listed. I know I'm going to achieve everything.

Every day I sit in my office chair where I can see all these things on the wall. I read them and look at the pictures before I do anything else. Several times during the day I look at them, and at the end of the day I ask myself, "Did I achieve all the things I wanted to," or "Did I do all the right things to help me achieve those goals?" If I didn't, then I know I've got to do something a little bit differently the next day.

Key point

Everything goes back to what you believe. If your belief level isn't there--if you truly don't believe you can achieve your goal, you won't. I think it was Henry Ford who said, **"If you think you can or you think you can't, you're right."** You've got to be in the mindset that you can achieve what you want to, so you can and you will. If you can't feel yourself in the moment, you won't ever know what it's like to be in the moment, so you can't move toward the goal of being in the moment. You create what happens to you in your future.

Herman is a Certified Identity Theft Risk Management Specialist who owns IDT Consultants. He is a speaker and trainer, not only for his own company but also for network marketing companies across the country. He is considered one of the top network marketers in the United States and is reachable on Facebook (facebook.com) under his name, "Herman Luette" and via his email at hluette@databreachexperts.com. His company website is www.DataBreachExperts.com.

Life And Business Success Principles:

Tony Ash

My Background

I had a life-changing experience when I was 19. My brother and I were very, very close. He and I bought a company from our family, then he died unexpectedly. That was a terrible time in my life, but I picked myself up, sold the company back to my family, and at 19 joined the United States Navy. Up to then I had kind of breezed through life. Things hadn't necessarily come easy, but I didn't have to work as hard as some people had to. I think I later figured out why. Prior to my brother's death I was always very positive.

Everybody has a tipping point or an epiphany or a light that turns on--whatever adage you want to use. With people who are successful, something has created that, and for me, it was something tragic.

My Affirmation Story

When I joined the Navy I excelled and gained rank as fast as I possibly could, and was given leadership over 235 electricians on an aircraft carrier. It was amazing that those who were working for me were, in some cases, 10 years older than I, but age had nothing to do with it. They wanted to be around someone who was very positive, and I've led my life like that.

It's not luck. I've learned that we put ourselves in those positions. How do you put yourself in that position? By becoming a very positive person.

I never thought about affirmations. I'm not one of those people who taped something to my mirror that said, "I'm going to be Chief Operating Officer for a company," or "I'm going to run a 50 million-dollar company." I used a slightly different approach. Probably the biggest thing I did is that **I believed in myself.**

People want to be around positive people and they want to be around successful people. Figure out the things that make you happy or things you feel you have an ability for. In business I work with a management philosophy and a thought process of figuring out what each person needs so I can help them be a better person. I believe that if people believe in themselves they're going to do a better job, be a better person, have a better home life, and come to work happier. They're going to want to come to work because they're positive and believe in what you're telling them. The thing I teach my folks is that I believe in you and I'm going to help you believe in yourself. A lot of people in management, middle management, even senior management aren't confident in their abilities.

My Affirmation Tools

I work with my people to teach them to believe in themselves, and I point out things they're really good at. I select a specific attribute someone has and say "You're awesome!" I'll say there are other managers who would love to have you with the abilities you have, which could be, for instance, the ability to foresee manufacturing problems. I hope I'm instilling that belief in others, and once they realize "I am pretty good," it's as if they come out of the fog and see the light. It's amazing what happens when people believe in themselves.

In the last year that I've been working with this current group of people, their absentee rate has dropped tremendously, sick days have dropped tremendously, and I know that's not just luck. I know it's because we've worked to instill positive beliefs and positive attitudes, and **good stuff is contagious.** I truly believe that a positive attitude rolls downhill. You're not going to find a president or a chief operating officer or a vice president of a company who sees the glass half empty.

Happiness is a choice. I know a lot of people who are miserable. Money and success have nothing to do with how they feel. I know people who have no money who are exceedingly happy, and I know multi-multi-millionaires who are the most unhappy people there are. Happiness is a choice, and I think that living a positive life is a choice as well. A long, long time ago I chose to be positive, and rarely do I allow myself to get down.

We've also got to be passionate about what we do. Passion is one of the things I know I personally have. It too is contagious.

People want to be around successful people and positive energy. We've all seen the naysayers who suck the life out of you, the negative people. I choose not to be around those folks in my personal life. I choose to be around those who typically are happy, positive people.

At the end of the day, what makes the difference, I think, is the positive thought, the energy from believing in yourself, the energy you give yourself to believe in yourself. Regardless of whether you say it internally or don't say it, or write it down or don't write it down--it doesn't matter. The end result is the same. **If you don't believe in it, if you don't believe in yourself, it's not going to happen.**

Key point
One of the things anybody can start with is to simply change your attitude. It doesn't matter what you do or who you are--you can change your attitude tomorrow. You truly can. You can have the same positive approach to life and the same passion regardless of what you do or how much you make.

Tony is an executive who can be reached on Facebook (facebook.com) under "TonyAsh"

Next Steps

Congratulations on completing *Dynamic Affirmations.* You've worked through the process. Now what?

Imagine if you had one resource you could count on to continue receiving support for your affirmations, and to network with people on the same journey as you, creating the results you've always wanted.

As a special thank you for reading *Dynamic Affirmations: Learn to Live the Law of Attraction with Purpose and Passion!*, Jodi Santangelo offers free access to the membership site www.Create Affirmations.com.

If you are still working toward getting 100 percent results from your affirmations, you'll want to sign up now! Here's what you can take advantage of:

- Read true stories from real people who have used affirmations successfully, even though some of them didn't believe in affirmations until discovering the tools that work for them.

- Get help with your affirmations online.

- Discover an abundance of methods that work for others, among which you'll find the most effective for you, too.

- Download and listen at your leisure to audio interviews from real people who've successfully used the tools revealed in *Dynamic Affirmations*.

- Share your own stories in our supportive, welcoming online community at www.Create Affirmations.com.

- Get sample "*Dynamic Affirmations*." Whatever you seek-- Prosperity and Abundance, Success, Love and Relationships, Health, or Overall Well-Being--you'll find helpful samples of "*Dynamic Affirmations*." One or more will resonate with you or help you jumpstart your own creative affirmation writing.

- Find a wealth of resources to move your affirmations forward faster in all areas of your life.

- Tell us your own *Dynamic Affirmation* Success Story that developed from the tools you learned and applied in this book for a chance to win one of our drawings!

If you're serious about your life and business and hope to attract what you really want, go now to www.CreateAffirmations.com/Bonus and sign up--free!

I'll meet you there.

Final Thoughts
Wow! What a Journey!

In 1997 I was fortunate to have learned the power of the Law of Attraction. I intentionally applied the attraction effect to create *Dynamic Affirmations* and today I'm in excellent health and very happy with life and my career of helping others.

You've reached the end of this book and learned some easy lessons on how the attraction effect works. You've discovered how creating *Dynamic Affirmations* can help you get more of what *you* want.

I suggest you revisit the positive statements, goals and affirmations you recorded in Part I and compare the results to your newly created affirmations. Notice how your affirmations now feel true for you and believable to you.

Remember, life is a process through which we grow and change every day. It's important to revisit your affirmations from time to time to ensure they are still working for you. If they are working, great! Keep doing what you are doing.

If not, you can always refer to this book for guidance. You can also make use of all the resources found on my websites:

www.CreateAffirmations.com
www.JodiSantangelo.com

Take the *Dynamic Affirmations* of yours that *feel really good*, and give them your attention and positive energy. The Law of Attraction (which is always checking) will respond by bringing you more of what you want in your business and your life.

I wish you well and challenge you to live your life each and every day "on purpose" and "with passion" by proactively tapping into the Law of Attraction.

May all your affirmations come true!

Jodi

About The Author

Until 1997 Jodi never knew what an affirmation was. As a kid she was happy-go-lucky and things seemed to naturally go her way. In 1997 a series of events, including a serious illness, got her attention. It was then she learned about affirmations, though she found most she created weren't effective for her. During her journey to wellness Jodi also discovered the powerful Law of Attraction and used it to turn her life around. She's been a student ever since.

During her experience as a District Governor with Toastmasters International she perfected the techniques to become an effective speaker and trainer, and combined these skills with her passion for teaching others to benefit from the attraction effect and creating *Dynamic Affirmations*.

Today, Jodi is a Certified Trainer and Coach and travels around the country inspiring audiences of all kinds. She's considered an exceptional facilitator delivering customized programs with high energy and enthusiasm. As an expert she is committed to helping people tap into the Law of Attraction and apply the proven principles to create the results they want in their business and their life.

To learn more about applying the Law of Attraction to your life, consider these opportunities:

Speaking Engagements:
To experience, live, the powerful positive energy Jodi Santangelo inspires in her audiences, invite her to facilitate a workshop or speak at your next event. Email Jodi@JodiSantangelo.com

Personal coaching:
For further details about one-on-one coaching, email Jodi@JodiSantangelo.com.

<u>Home Learning Programs:</u>
Additional resources are available at
<u>www.JodiSantangelo.com</u>

<u>www.CreateAffirmations.com</u>

<u>www.JodiSantangelo.com</u>

Additional Resources
For Personal Development

Eker, T. Harv, *Secrets of the Millionaire Mind*,
HarperCollins, 2005.

Grabhorn, Lynn, *Excuse Me, Your Life is Waiting
Playbook,* Hampton Roads Publishing, 2001.

Hay, Louise L., *You Can Heal Your Life,* Hay House,
Inc., 1999.

Learning Strategies, www.LearningStrategies.com

Losier, Michael J., *Law of Attraction: the Science of
Attracting More of What You Want and Less of What
You Don't,* Wellness Central Edition, 2003, 2006.

For free Internet marketing resources from the World's
#1 Internet Wealth Advocate, check out Stephen Pierce's
blog at www.dtalpha.com

BUY A SHARE OF THE FUTURE IN YOUR COMMUNITY

These certificates make great holiday, graduation and birthday gifts that can be personalized with the recipient's name. The cost of one S.H.A.R.E. or one square foot is $54.17. The personalized certificate is suitable for framing and will state the number of shares purchased and the amount of each share, as well as the recipient's name. The home that you participate in "building" will last for many years and will continue to grow in value.

HABITAT FOR HUMANITY

THIS CERTIFIES THAT
YOUR NAME HERE
HAS INVESTED IN A HOME FOR A DESERVING FAMILY

1985-2005

TWENTY YEARS OF BUILDING FUTURES IN OUR
COMMUNITY ONE HOME AT A TIME

1200 SQUARE FOOT HOUSE @ $65,000 = $54.17 PER SQUARE FOOT
This certificate represents a tax deductible donation. It has no cash value.

Here is a sample SHARE certificate:

YES, I WOULD LIKE TO HELP!

I support the work that Habitat for Humanity does and I want to be part of the excitement! As a donor, I will receive periodic updates on your construction activities but, more importantly, I know my gift will help a family in our community realize the dream of homeownership. **I would like to SHARE in your efforts against substandard housing in my community!** *(Please print below)*

PLEASE SEND ME _____ SHARES at $54.17 EACH = $ $_____

In Honor Of: _____

Occasion: (Circle One) HOLIDAY   BIRTHDAY   ANNIVERSARY

  OTHER: _____

Address of Recipient: _____

Gift From: _____ *Donor Address:* _____

Donor Email: _____

I AM ENCLOSING A CHECK FOR $ $_____ PAYABLE TO HABITAT FOR HUMANITY **OR** PLEASE CHARGE MY VISA OR MASTERCARD *(CIRCLE ONE)*

Card Number _____ Expiration Date: _____

Name as it appears on Credit Card _____ Charge Amount $ _____

Signature _____

Billing Address _____

Telephone # Day _____ Eve _____

PLEASE NOTE: Your contribution is tax-deductible to the fullest extent allowed by law.
Habitat for Humanity • P.O. Box 1443 • Newport News, VA 23601 • 757-596-5553
www.HelpHabitatforHumanity.org